George H. Howard

A Guide in the Theory and Practice of Mechanism in Pianoforte Playing

George H. Howard

A Guide in the Theory and Practice of Mechanism in Pianoforte Playing

ISBN/EAN: 9783337019396

Printed in Europe, USA, Canada, Australia, Japan

Cover: Foto ©Thomas Meinert / pixelio.de

More available books at **www.hansebooks.com**

Theory and Practice of Mechanism

— IN —

PIANO-FORTE PLAYING.

By G. H. HOWARD, A. M.

BATTLE CREEK, MICH.
REVIEW AND HERALD STEAM PRINT.
1883.

TO

JOHN W. TUFTS,

OF BOSTON, MASSACHUSETTS,

To whose invaluable instruction, counsel, and example,

I OWE SO MUCH,

THIS WORK IS GRATEFULLY DEDICATED.

PREFACE.

THIS little work is not wholly new in its purpose. Plaidy and others have treated the subject of Technique with more or less attention to formulation of principles involved, but such formulation has too frequently been incomplete and illogical, if not absolutely false. The result has been, in a large number of instances, that the most arduous practice has resulted only in disappointment, failure, or physical injury to the hand. It may be well believed that a more exact presentation of the fundamental principles of Technique will be invaluable to many teachers and pianists. The teacher's labor may be greatly lightened, and the range and result of his work be much extended, by means of a well-defined method. The future artist thereby economizes valuable time, which may consequently be applied to the higher ends of musical art. The complete virtuoso, even, never disregards the minutest particular which may add to the precision of his skill or the resource of his power.

This work is prepared merely as an outline of the subject. It was written at the urgent request of pupils, but in the midst of other and very pressing duties, and in consequence

the subject could not receive full justice. It will, nevertheless, I trust, be found somewhat more comprehensive than
other works upon this subject which have hitherto appeared.

This Outline is offered to the public in the hope that it
may advance the cultivation of true pianism, by systemizing
and therefore economizing the labor of teacher and pianist.
The excellent results already attained by a few who have had
the benefit of the work while in manuscript, lead me to hope
that it may meet with a favorable reception from all unpreju-
diced minds and faithful workers.

G. H. H.

PRELIMINARY REMARKS.

A FREQUENT cause of failure in developing mechanical skill in playing the piano may be found in the almost universal neglect of the theory of Technique. It is a subject at present nearly uninvestigated. When one is thoroughly acquainted with *causes* and *means*, little difficulty need be encountered in securing true *effects* and solid *results*. One may, with fair application, be absolutely certain of fine attainments in Technique; and instead of ninety per cent of failures to ten per cent of successes, success might be the *rule*, and failure the rare exception; especially if musical training were always to embrace the necessary concurrent discipline and culture of the powers of the soul, the intellect, the sensibilities, the will, the nerves, muscles, tendons, and ligaments. At present, in too many cases, the sensibilities, the nerves, and muscles only, are cultivated or brought into training; and the sensibilities are so imperfectly cultivated, that they only stimulate or call into exercise the passions instead of the soul and spirit. The nerves and muscles are so inadequately trained, that they act with a mechanical, forced obedience, and not as willing, inspired agents of the all-commanding will.

Intelligence is the source of all motion, order, and control; hence any adequate comprehension of the laws of Technique demands a never-failing regard for the offices of the mental and vital forces required in its development. The soul and mind must always be the creator and executor in musical performance. The hands, arms, muscles, nerves, etc., are only the tools, or instruments, which the mind employs. The soul creates at least a conception, whether in extempore or interpretative musical art. Without the soul and intellect, no position could be maintained, no motion directed or controlled. The will might, indeed, act independently, but not consciously, and therefore not effectively. This is the condition of those who train only nerves, muscles, passions, or sensibilities in musical studies. In this Outline, therefore, the offices of the soul and mind in the study and practice of Technique will not be overlooked, or for a moment lost sight of.

THE METHOD.

In studying, practicing, or teaching Technique, it is unsafe, as a rule, to take up an exercise for *practice* first, then to deduce the principles which it illustrates, and then investigate the mental processes necessary. The true method is to take up first the analysis and the study of the mental and mechanical processes required, then to proceed to the deduction of the principles, to the application of the analysis or analyses,* and to the practice of the exercise.

This process may be reversed in exceptional cases. *Some* persons of an ardent nervous temperament, and of quick perceptive, rather than strong and deep reflective faculties, will accomplish more to take up the practice first, the analysis and theory afterward. With such temperaments, the teacher should give the exercise first, then conduct the analysis, then obtain the statement of underlying principles, and lastly enter upon the investigation of the mental processes required. Even intellectually cultivated persons are often strangely disinclined to these studies, but they are *more vitally important*, even, for them than any other class, and must be insisted on.

---

* Examples of Analysis of Mechanism are given in subsequent pages.

A pupil who has been trained previously in dependence on exclusively mechanical exercises, and who is unable to classify positions, motions, accents, and forces away from the piano and from the music-page, should be trained for weeks or months in this study, apart from the requisite practice.

THE TRUE IDEAL OF TECHNICAL TRAINING.

The true ideal of technical training is that of intelligent efforts and careful discipline leading to sure and exact results. Corrections of position, motion, or touch, are to a very great extent unnecessary; and *when* necessary, detract seriously from one's success. When they must be made, they should be prepared for by a careful restatement of the principles of position, motion, or touch, which are involved, thus preparing for a better comprehension, and a true instead of false action of the will. A false habit must not be allowed to linger. Wrong tendencies may be destroyed at once and right tendencies established in their place. The habits may be, and often are, revolutionized in an hour's effort of teacher and pupil. This can occur when the heart, mind, and soul are all enlisted. The power of *good* is infinite, the power of evil is infinitesimal; therefore, *a right habit in its actual inception has a power to establish itself which a wrong habit, after* YEARS *of growth, can never possess.* This important truth is full of encouragement to those who have unwittingly fallen into bad habits. Others will seek good and avoid errors, for the sake of good and the experience of its power. Conscientiousness in the practice and study for the development of Technique, are the strength of the soul in its experiences of the power of music.

TECHNIQUE.

A TECHNIQUE which shall be perfectly available for the demands of artistic performance, requires attention to four principal departments:—

1. POSITION.   3. MOTION.
2. TENSION.   4. APPLICATION OF FORCE.

1. POSITION.

1. Position is the relationship of one part to another. It may relate first to the general position of the body, embracing also the height of seat, and distance from the instrument. The general position should be unconstrained, but never indolent in the smallest degree.

The player should seek to cultivate passivity in the nerves and muscles, remembering that they are the servants of an intelligent will. They must be in readiness for an instant obedience to its mandates. To *maintain* this condition of perfect passivity is often a difficult matter. It is, indeed, an impossibility in most cases, without careful attention and excellent training. It depends upon a sufficient and proper tension and relief of tension. Any crossing of the feet or placing them under the seat, or extending them fully, should be avoided. Likewise should any sinking or drooping of the chest be avoided. The other extreme, of throwing the head and shoulders back of the perpendicular, is equally bad. A gracefully erect position, and what is known as the active chest by some vocalists (that is, a position admitting of a full expansion of the lungs), should be maintained. Free and full respiration is of the utmost importance for any good physical action, and it is *indispensable* for the brain, if it would conceive, create, and direct with its native energy. One who spends a third of his life at the piano, as so many music students do, must cultivate a good position, or suffer in health seriously, and despair of attaining either a fine Technique or fine interpretative power. With strong and free pulses feeding the active brain, one may maintain through the exercises of pianism, a splendid state of health, provided hygienic conditions be not wholly disregarded. These exercises are as valuable for the health as any gymnastic exercises, in quickening the circulation, equalizing the nervous forces, developing the muscles, and stimulating and strengthening the brain. Ecstacy is the only word capable of describing one's condition after a good faithful hour's practice.

HEIGHT.

The height of the seat for the performer should be such that the elbows shall be from one to three inches above the level of the key-board. (This height must be conformed to the requirements of the relationship of the fingers, hand, and arm, but will be between the limits above specified.) Small children, or very small adults, may find that this arrangement prevents them from reaching the floor with their feet. In such cases, the feet must have some other support, and when it becomes necessary to use the pedals (which should rarely be allowed for the first year or two of instruction), the pedals must be extended by some mechanical contrivance.

THE SEAT.

The pupil must sit fairly upon the seat, never on the edge of it merely. The seat *should* be of a construction better than any now in use, and a demand for such a one should be created. It should be broad and firm, and provided with a back high enough to support the entire spine up to the neck.

The seat should be adjustable to any height which may be required. The construction should, nevertheless, be simple and strong.*

THE DISTANCE.

The distance of the performer from the piano, should conform to the required relationship of the arm and body. The arm should be so extended that the elbow shall be from two to four inches forward of the perpendicular line of the body. Four inches would be an extreme.

Concerning the general position, the height, and the distance, the judgment must take cognizance of, and be duly exercised by, the sensations experienced. It is the office of the sensor nerves (nerves of sensation) to inform the mind of the qualities of the relationships of muscles and motor nerves. It thereby becomes conscious of the power of the muscles and nerves to perform their offices to the finest particular and nicest adjustment, which the will regulates with most delicate precision.

The rules above given for position, height, and distance, are of little more than general use, unless one learns early to realize relationships and conditions of motor nerves and muscles, through observation of the sensor nerves and the sensations they impart. The more perfect this inner consciousness can become, the greater the certainty and freedom in Technique.

DISCIPLINE IN POSITION.

The pupil should be trained in taking a correct and graceful position before passing to the other exercises. The position should be constantly observed and criticised in the minutest particulars by the teacher. He should strive not only to secure good results, but also to lay the foundations for future good habits, by inducing, through good instruc-

---

* Since the above was written, the manufacture of a Piano Stool answering very nearly to the above requirements has been begun in Buffalo, N. Y.

tion, suggestion, and discipline, a power of reflection and discrimination, which of themselves are the most prolific *sources* of good results.

2. Position of the hand. The back of the hand, with the third section of the finger (that nearest the hand), should form a line horizontal with the forearm. The first section of each finger should be perpendicular to the key, the second section at an angle of twenty-two degrees. The thumb should be extended so that the second or middle section shall be parallel to the frame of the hand; the third section turning outward, at an angle of ten degrees; the first section turning inward, at an angle of ten degrees.

The height of the hand should be proportionately equal in all its parts. This being established, the thumb will be at an oblique angle with the surface on which it rests. This relationship is an important one, and is too often overlooked or ignored. By a proper regard for it, a better control of the thumb may be obtained than is possible otherwise.

HOW TO OVERCOME A FALSE TENDENCY.

Some persons have a tendency to turn the thumbs outward when the fingers are properly curved. This arises from undue contraction of muscles controlling the thumb, and may be overcome by attentive and careful effort. With beginners or with advanced pupils, the process must be the same in overcoming any false tendency. Seek to avoid it in its inception; prevent the beginnings of error; thus it is shorn of its power. Avoid errors, not by greater but by more intelligent efforts of the will. Intelligence, comprehension, and consciousness may lead one directly to the results desired, and good habits may immediately supplant those which are bad.

TWO WAYS OF TAKING THE POSITION.

Two ways of taking the position may be employed.

FIRST METHOD. Hold the arm in a horizontal line, and extend the hand and fingers in the same line. Then bend the first and second sections of the fingers to the angles required.* Then bend the thumb to the required angles. Lastly, regulate the transverse poise of the hand to the horizontal line, and the sides of the fingers to the perpendicular. This is the most useful exercise, and should be practiced daily from one to eight weeks. The control is often secured with difficulty, and many persons cannot preserve it without long practice.

SECOND METHOD. The second method is often useful, though never so valuable as the first. Let the arm and hand be extended horizontally upon a table, resting passively upon it. Then raise arm and hand slightly, and carry them one or two inches from the body, *forward*, allowing the fingertips still to rest upon the table, but also allowing them to roll enough to admit of the fingers assuming their required angles. Then move the thumb and form it in its required angles, allowing it still to rest upon the table. Lastly, regulate the transverse poise of the hand, and the sides of the fingers to the perpendicular with the surface of the table.

PRACTICE OF THE POSITIONS.

The positions should be practiced first with the two hands in alternation ten or fifteen times, studying with minute exactness the adjustment of every part, and seeking to obtain the most accurate relationships. A difference of an eighth of an inch may be a most important one, and may cause the difference between control and lack of control, or between ease and constraint.

Those who do not neglect the study of position, but per-

*See page 14, "Form of Fingers."

severe in it to the satisfaction of the faithful teacher, may
know that thereby they lay a foundation for a Technique not
merely excellent, but absolutely perfect. It is unfailing.
Embarrassment or nervousness cannot rob one of it. The
study of position is of vital importance. It must extend
through years of training. Without it, no success is attained
that is thoroughly worthy of the name. It is, therefore, of
the utmost importance that it should be carefully studied
from the beginning. Conscientiousness in practice contrib-
utes to spiritual power, on which power of conception depends.

2. TENSION.

DEFINITION.—Tension is force of will, greater or less, applied to any cord, tendon, ligament, muscle, or nerve, for
the purpose of maintaining a position or causing a motion.

An increase or decrease of tension is required by changes
of positions or motions. Exquisite judgment in regulating the
tension and adapting it to its required ends, may be attained
by careful study and observation. The sensor nerves assist
one greatly in this study. One may attain such certainty of
judgment in adapting the tension, as to usually anticipate the
exact amount demanded at every change. Yet this is not
always possible, for many modifying circumstances are to be
taken into account, so numerous are the conditions by which
its requirements are affected.

EXERCISE OF TENSION.

Elementary exercise in tension is obtained in taking and
retaining a position, especially the latter. Holding the arm
and hand in position give good exercise in tension.

FIRST SERIES, WITH SLIGHTEST TENSION NECESSARY TO
MAINTAIN POSITION.

1. Hold right hand in position ten seconds, and left
hand same. Repeat five times.

2. Right hand in position fifteen seconds; left hand, the same. Repeat five times.

3. Right hand in position twenty-five seconds; left hand, the same. Repeat five times.

SECOND SERIES, WITH STRONGER TENSION.

1. The position may be retained fifteen seconds with a higher degree of tension.
2. Twenty seconds.
3. Forty seconds.

THIRD SERIES, WITH STRONGEST TENSION.

1. Position retained twenty-five seconds.
2. Position retained forty seconds.
3. Position retained one minute.

ITS RELATION TO THE SUBJECT OF POSITION.

This subject is so intimately related to that of position, that it will be constantly referred to in the analysis of position.

A change of tension in motor nerves and muscles, causes motion. These changes of tension must be observed and studied in all complete analysis of motion.

The study of tension may be pursued further in connection with the study of motion.

3. MOTION.

The laws of motion in piano-forte-playing have been only partially generalized, except in a few instances; they have not been completely detailed in any published work. A complete classification of motions required in playing is as indispensable as the classification of words in the study of grammar.

REQUISITES OF ALL MOTION.

MENTAL REQUISITES. All motion has three principal mental requisites:—

2

1. CORRECT APPREHENSION.   2. TRUE JUDGMENT.
3. PRECISE DIRECTION.

A right understanding (*i. e.*, correct apprehension) of a motion is plainly enough the first condition of accuracy. True judgment in reference to the amount and kind of motion used, is equally important as it insures an exact application of the laws of Technique. A precise direction is dependent upon an intelligent action of the will. The teacher should seek to train the pupil in all these mental exercises.

MECHANICAL REQUISITES.

The mechanical requisites of motion are the following:—

1. CAPACITY.   3. INDEPENDENCE.
2. PRECISION.   4. FACILITY.

Capacity exists whenever the hand, arm, or body have no defects which interfere with the employment of the parts required in playing.

Precision depends on readiness of disposition, mental application, and on discipline.

Independence and *Facility* are very rarely the gifts of nature, except in a small degree, and depend upon careful training and persevering practice.

Independence is the power of each finger, hand, or arm to move by itself, without affecting or influencing any other part, even in the direction of a similar motion, or a compensating pressure, tension, or contraction. Independence may also be the power of each member to act in opposite movement to some other, each movement being perfectly directed. A similar movement is in some circumstances, more difficult, and requires greater independence than a contrary movement. Independence must be sought for in perfection of quality and amplitude of quantity.

Facility consists in ease of motion and instantaneous obedience to the will. It is dependent on flexibility and suppleness, gained through methodical and unremitting practice. Facility must always be subordinated to accuracy and independence. Where this order is reversed, carelessness, confusion in method, and even faults in rendering, quickly follow.

GENERAL CLASSIFICATION OF MOTIONS.

Motions are Primary or Principal, and Auxiliary. Principal, or Primary Motions are those which are employed in the act of taking or leaving keys. All others are Auxiliary Motions.

FINGER ACTION.

First in order comes the study and practice of the motion of the fingers, usually called Finger Action. This has, in technical exercise, three elements. The Upward Motion, the Point of Repose in Space, and the Downward Motion.

The mechanical requisites of finger action are four in number (in addition to the requisites of all motion before specified). They are Unity, Directness, Steadiness, and Impulsiveness. In other words, the finger action must be a motion of the finger in which all parts move together, and in which it moves directly, steadily, and yet with an impulse quick and exact enough to produce the tone desired.

The thumb should move from the joint where it is connected with the hand, usually about an inch from the wrist. Observe that the structure of the thumb is quite similar to that of the fingers. Many imperfect players seem never to have discovered that it has three sections as the fingers have.

The fingers should move from the joint where they are connected with the hand. As they have different powers and different tendencies, the conditions of their training must be different, yet with uniform results in view. The second and fifth fingers have opposite tendencies with most persons, therefore the technical treatment must be opposite, if uniform results are reached. The second finger is naturally so free in its movements (from common uses), that when un-

trained, it communicates its motion to, and affects the whole
hand; while the fifth finger is so weak and stubborn in the
hand-joint (from *neglect* in common uses), that it can scarcely
produce a clear tone by its own motion alone.   Hence the
one finger requires restraint in motion, and the other freedom in motion, by which method uniformity and equalization are reached.

Great difficulty is generally experienced in the use of the
fourth finger, and the nature of this difficulty is unlike that
of the others.   This needs special training for the quality of
independence.   The third finger needs, usually, less repression than the second, as regards motion, but more repression
as regards force.

THE PRACTICE.—EXERCISE OF SINGLE FINGERS.

Let the fingers be exercised in their motions on the table,
all rules of position being first observed.   A correct position
being assumed, the upward movement (the first element) may
be given, observing the four requisites of motion, each one
being examined in successive motions.   Or again, the finger
may be exercised as prescribed five or ten times, for the
attainment of unity, and the same number of times for
directness, steadiness, and impulsiveness.

Then follows the study of the second element (which is
indispensable for the individualization of the motions), the
point of repose.   Here observe the relationship of all the
parts, that correct position may be established.   The repose
should occupy for this purpose, from five to ten seconds the
first two or three days of practice.   Then practice for union
of the four requisites of motion, together or separately, in
connection with the object of attaining correct position or
relationship at the point of repose.

The third element, the downward motion, may then be
practiced, first *by itself*, for the attainment of accuracy in the

four requisites (in many cases practicing for them separately), afterward *in connection* with the other two elements.

From one to four weeks of continuous, daily practice, may often be given with profit to the study of finger motion. Some persons have, with decided benefit, practiced these exercises for months. The smallest amount of practice which would be productive, would be thirty movements per day with each finger. Let the hands alternate frequently.

EXERCISES OF TWO OR MORE FINGERS IN CONNECTION.

In like manner, two or more fingers may be exercised in connection and succession. The first and second, second and third, third and fourth, fourth and fifth; then the first and third, second and fourth, third and fifth; then first and fourth, second and fifth, and first and fifth may be used. Let it be understood that no force or pressure is required in all this practice; they should at first be avoided. Study first the precision, then for increase of motion and independence, and afterward, if these have been well established, effort may be made for a little facility. The fourth finger needs especially careful training, for the attainment of a sufficient independence. It must never be overworked in the smallest degree. It must not be forced, but gently though effectually exercised. It should be so passive that it will be in readiness to obey the slightest promptings of the will.

APPLICATION OF FINGERS TO KEY-BOARD.

The application of fingers to the key-board is the next point in order. This should be made in such a manner that all previous rules of position shall be perfectly observed. It then should be noticed that each finger has a specific point* or spot upon its key which it should retain when in repose,

---

*Usually as follows: The thumb the depth of the nail on the keys; the second finger a quarter of an inch from the black keys; the third finger an eighth of an inch from the same; the fourth a third of an inch, and the fifth same as thumb. Each finger midway between sides of keys.

and from which and toward which it should directly tend when in motion. Deviations should be carefully guarded against.

EXERCISE OF SINGLE FINGER IN PRODUCTION OF TONE.

If the training in position, motion, and tension has been well conducted to this point, a certain kind of artistic sense has been awakened. This may now at once be kindled into life which finds its highest experience in artistic production. Here the will, intellect, and sensibilities are all brought into operation. The sense of perfection or beauty of tone is in the soul. The power to create motion lies in the will. All judgment concerning these processes of thought, action, and experience is in the intellect.

4. APPLICATION OF FORCE.

In addition to the weight of the finger, the muscles and nerves must carry or propel the weight of the key. The application of force here required, is the product of an imperceptibly increased tension above what has been used in previous exercises, and a slight increase of impulsiveness in motion.

TONE.—PRODUCTION OR FORMATION OF TONE.

A tone in its outward form has three features: a point of articulation or utterance, a period of duration, and a point of termination. Each of these elements must in practice be made distinct and separate,—this is the beginning of clearness in execution. With this, all passage-playing, however rapid, may be perfectly intelligible and pure.

QUANTITY AND QUALITY OF TONE.

Quantity and Quality of Tone must here receive due attention, adapting them to the strength of the finger and the requirements of its training. Fine discrimination on the part of the teacher is here required.

DURATION OF TONE.

From three to ten seconds should be given to each tone that the principles of performance may be duly realized and fully carried out. *Absolute precision* must be attained. All necessity for corrections *must be avoided*.

PRESSURE OF THE KEY.

The key must of course be held with a nice adjustment of pressure, neither too great nor too little, but enough for the perfect retention of the tone.

MECHANICAL ELEMENTS FOR PRODUCTION OF TONE.

It will thus be observed that as the formation of a tone has three elements, so the mechanical means of its production has three elements. The striking, the holding, and the releasing of the key. The releasing of the key should be effected with great elasticity of motion, yet excess in this particular is to be avoided. Fifty movements per day at least, should be prescribed, unless a danger of overworking the muscles and nerves be thereby incurred. Too much work is as bad as too little. The nerves and muscles should be kept in a condition of freshness.

TWO-NOTE EXERCISES.

Practice with successive fingers in the employment of two-note exercises may be undertaken at the beginning of the second or third week of instruction. The following principles should be presented, and the analysis of the mechanism should be made before the practice is begun.

THE LEGATO TOUCH.

At this point careful attention to the connection of the tones is demanded for the cultivation of what is termed the *legato touch.* This consists in retaining each tone until the next is produced. This necessitates retaining each key until after (an *instant* after) the next is taken. This allows time for the operation of the machinery of the piano.

CULTURE OF THE EAR.

The ear must be trained to the consciousness of the connection of tone. This can be done by listening to the vibration which follows the percussion, and observing the instant when the succeeding tone meets the ear; at that instant the preceding tone should cease. It is better that the tones blend a little rather than that they should fail to meet, and thus fall short of connection. With sufficient prolongation of the tone, and with attentive listening, the legato touch may be established at this point in all its perfection.

AVOIDANCE OF FALSE RELATIONSHIPS.

In two-note exercises, care must be taken anew that the fingers do not draw up the hand as they are raised. The point of repose in space should be improved to examine the relationship. A false relationship must not, however, be corrected; the movement producing the relationship must be given anew with the avoidance of the disturbing cause. Each tone should occupy from one to ten seconds. Slow practice is the true and sure road to success.

ANALYSIS OF THE TWO-NOTE EXERCISE, C. D., C. D., ETC., WITH REFERENCE TO MECHANISM.

1. Preparatory upward movement of first finger (thumb). 2. Point of repose. 3. Downward motion and production of the tone C. 4. Pressure of the key and prolongation of the tone. 5. Upward motion of second finger. 6. Point of repose. 7. Downward action and production of tone D. 8. Pressure of key and prolongation of tone D. 9. Upward movement for the release of first finger and its key, and termination of the tone C. 10. Point of repose for first finger. 11. Downward movement of first finger and production of tone C. 12. Pressure of key. 13. Upward

movement of second finger for termination of tone D, etc. This exercise should have from twenty-five to seventy-five repetitions daily.

A PLAN FOR A COURSE OF LESSONS.

Let it be understood that although Technique is occupy-ing our entire attention, the lessons should embrace from the earliest moment, other departments. A scheme somewhat as follows, will be found practicable,—courses of study always depending on capacity, intellectual attainments, etc.

FIRST LESSON.—TECHNIQUE.

Instruction in Position, Height, Distance, etc., and exer-cises in Position, Tension, and Motion.

SECOND LESSON.—THE SCALE, NAMES OF KEYS, OCTAVES, AND NOTATION.

Instruction in formation of Scale, its tones and intervals. Names of Keys, names of Octaves,* Lines, and Spaces. Treble Clef. Names of Notes, etc.

THIRD LESSON.—TECHNIQUE.

Exercise of single and two fingers. Continued exercises in Position and Tension. Application of fingers to keys.

FOURTH LESSON.—READING.

Representation of particular keys by particular notes. Exercises in reading notes orally.

FIFTH LESSON.—TECHNIQUE.

Exercises for three fingers. Continued exercises in Posi-tion and Motion.

With two lessons per week, a scheme on the basis above suggested, may be carried out for some years. Some pupils should advance even more slowly than the above scheme would indicate, as it is never to be admitted that they shall

---

*See Diagram.

pass to a succeeding exercise before the preceding is duly perfected.

THREE, FOUR, AND FIVE-NOTE EXERCISES.

For six months, a year, or two years, two, three, four, and five-note exercises may be used with profit. (See Plaidy's Technical Studies for examples of these exercises.) The three, four, and five note exercises require greater steadiness of the hand, and a correspondingly greater tension is required in holding the hand. This need not, however, degenerate into undue contraction and stiffness.

These exercises should be carefully analyzed, that the pupil may become well disciplined in analysis, and the observation of every mechanical element.

TRANSPOSITIONS.

They should be transposed into one key after another; the theory of transposition being presented after the theory of the structure of the scale has been made familiar. (See page 29.) The application and location of the fingers should be as nearly as possible the same in all keys; but the slight differences necessary should be determined and specified by the teacher. The key of G is mechanically the same as the key of C, as it has no black key in the compass of the first five keys. No transposition into G is therefore called for, unless desirable for the sake of a different sound. On this principle the following transpositions are all which are necessary in Major keys:—

From C to key of D.

From C to key of E, to key of B, to key of F♯.

From C to key of C♯, to key of E♭, to key of B♭.

From C to key of F.

Transpositions into Minor keys should be made on the same principle. They can be easily selected.

Exercises with accidentals may prove very useful, if a complete analysis of the elements of position and motion be made.

The analysis of such an exercise as this—

should specify the necessary slight change in the curvature, and the extension of the fourth finger in preparation for taking the key F sharp, and its resumption of its preceding form in preparation for the following F natural.

ACCENT.

The more facility gained and fluency acquired, the more necessary will become the study of accent. Accent is to playing what emphasis is to speech. Its object is similar, and the method of its development similar.

It has also an additional use, which is that of defining groups and measures, thus rendering the playing intelligible, when it would otherwise be obscure.

The accent exercises introduced in a recent method, are indeed valuable, but not to be depended upon to that extent which the authors seem to do, for the general development of the touch or comprehension of rhythmic forms.

But they are useful in inducing elasticity of touch, and perfecting the equalization of the fingers; also, for aiding the habit of concentration and strengthening the power of conception. With these objects in view, five-note exercises should be practiced in groups of five, six, seven, eight, and nine, besides the more common groups of two, three, and four.

THE HIGHER TECHNICAL TRAINING FROM FIVE-NOTE EXERCISES.

Five-note exercises should at first be practiced very slowly, allowing from one to ten seconds for each note. Afterward, as precision is gained, fluency may be sought for, and a gradual increase in velocity may be attempted. Never practice faster, however, than you can play uninterruptedly and with ease and precision. The *tempo* in the more fluent or rapid movements may be regulated by the use of the metronome, not playing *with* the metronome, but in a certain degree of quickness as indicated by the metronome. Thus if the greatest practicable fluency through one week be $\digamma = 92$, the following week it may be increased to 104, the next to 112, the next to 116, and so on, or even with more gradual progress.

INCREASE OF POWER IN TOUCH.

The touch at first should be *m p* or *m*, but as strength is gained through use, the greater and lesser degrees of power should be studied. In the latter, the touch must not become inarticulate; but the tones, though subdued, must be pure and perfect: in the former they must not become unmusical, and the tones, though loud, may still remain tones, and not degenerate into noise.

PRACTICE FOR ENDURANCE AND MUSCULAR EXERCISE

Should be introduced at this stage for all but the strongest hands. For this purpose, fifty to one hundred repetitions of an exercise with fortissimo touch may be useful.

Exercises with holding tones, in repeated tones, and in moving figures, should be deferred, at least until after the practice of the Major and Minor scales has been carried through the first stage. In most cases they may be deferred to a point still later, through the first stage of simple arpeggios. Exercises with holding tones are useful, not for *securing* real independence, but for *increasing* it. Independence should be secured in the first practice of finger action. Exercises for fingers covering six keys as in Lebert and Stark's Method, Sec. 27, should be used.

THEORY AND PRACTICE OF SCALES.

The theory of scale forms should be presented and fully elucidated to the pupil before any attempt is made to examine into the theory of scale Technique. It should be presented in the same manner as in the study of general Musical Theory,* in which every piano teacher should be well versed, and which every student of the piano should pursue in connection with his practice.

A two years' course in vocal music is also to be recommended. The scale should be memorized so thoroughly that all the component tones of each scale may be unhesitatingly repeated, and the key mentioned from the signature, and the signature from the key, in Minor as well as in Major scales, also the relationships of Major to Minor scales, and Minor to Major scales.

THEORY OF SCALE FINGERINGS.

The theory of scale forms, *i. e.*, all forms of scales being fully understood, the theory of scale fingering will come next into review. To this point only five different keys have been used, one finger applying to each key. But in the scale even of one octave, eight keys are employed, and therefore the simple natural succession of the fingers is now impossible. The necessity for two or more applications is therefore obvious. The eighth key, bearing the same name as the first, is to be considered as the same key, and, though it be used for a concluding note, it is to be regarded also as the beginning of a new series, *i. e.*, a new octave, when an extended scale is required.

Therefore the scale consists of *seven representative keys*. These are divided into two groups: the first comprising three, the second group four keys, or *vice versa*. Let it be understood once for all that this grouping exists in all scales,

---

*See " Primer of Modern Musical Tonality," by J. H. Cornell, published by Schirmer, New York. $1.00.

though in a disguised form in some. The ready appreciation and realization of this grouping enables one to economize much time in practice, and more readily to attain certainty and facility in all passage playing, because then the finger locations are more readily and perfectly classified.

To the first group, the first three fingers are applied, in an ascending scale with the right hand, or in a descending scale with the left hand. To the second group, the first four fingers are applied in the before mentioned right hand and left hand scales. This order is reversed in the reverse direction of the scales. The fifth finger is used only for concluding keys.

Interruption in performing the scale is avoided and the tone-chain made perfect by means of auxiliary motions, yet to be specified.

The scale, like all five-note figures, is a finger exercise. The fingers take every key and produce every tone exclusively by their own motion. The use of auxiliary motions also renders the connections of tone possible between the groups, and affords convenience in passing from group to group.

AUXILIARY MOTIONS.

The Auxiliary Motions are the passing of the thumb under the hand and transfer (or carrying) of hand and arm. Turning the hand is also to be used to a small extent as an Auxiliary Motion. The passing of the thumb is subject (in slow synthetical practice) to two conditions: 1. Regulation as to direction. 2. Regulation as to time of motion.

REGULATION AS TO DIRECTION.

It should move in a strictly horizontal line from a medium point of elevation above the key. This point of elevation should not generally be less than an eighth, or more than a quarter of an inch above the key levels, unless unusual shortness or length of the fingers should require different conditions. The least space necessary is usually to be taken in order to avoid raising the hand, and thus throwing it out of position. The joint connecting the thumb with the hand must be stretched and made to yield so as to obviate as far as possible the necessity of turning the hand. The thumb should be so carried that it should keep its prescribed distance on the key.

REGULATION AS TO TIME OF MOTION.

The Regulation as to Time of Motion must always be made with a regard to the time of motion of the fingers. While the second finger is holding its key, the thumb should pass as far as the third key in the scale, and after the third finger has struck, and while it is holding its key, the thumb should pass as far as the fourth key, thus having the thumb always the distance of one key in advance of the finger which is in use.

COMPLETE ANALYSIS OF MECHANISM OF THE SCALE.

The Complete Analysis of the Mechanism of the Scale is as follows :—

1. Accuracy of position being secured, the upward movement of first finger (thumb). 2. Point of repose. 3. Action of thumb (for taking the tone). 4. Pressure sufficient for holding key. 5. Upward movement of second finger. 6. Point of repose. 7. Action of second finger. 8. Pressure of second finger. 9. Prompt upward movement of first finger (thumb), (for release of key) to medium elevation. 10. (N. B.) Passing of thumb distance of two keys to middle of third key. The raising and passing of the thumb should be distinct motions in all practice of the first week or month. 11. Upward movement of third finger. 12. Point of repose. 13. Action of third finger. 14. Pressure of third finger. 15. Prompt upward action of second finger for release of key. 16. Passing of thumb distance of one key to middle

of fourth. 17. Point of repose. 18. Slight upward movement (of thumb). 19. Action of thumb. 20. Pressure
with thumb. 21. Transfer of fingers, hand, and arm to new
location on fifth, sixth, seventh, and eighth keys. 22. Upward action of second finger. 23. Point of repose. 24.
Action of second finger, etc.

THE TENSION.

The tension of the large muscles of the arm is necessarily
somewhat greater in the scale than in Five-Note Exercises.
This should never degenerate into local contraction or stiffen-
ing. It is necessary in order to preserve steadiness in the
poise and in the carrying of the arm. The key preceding
the act of transfer should also be held a little more firmly
than the others, in order that the connection of tone may
not be lost at that point.

PRESSURE OF KEY AND TENSION.

The Pressure of Key and Tension should here be very
carefully adjusted so that they shall not detract in the least
(*as they need not*) from elasticity in the touch. Elasticity is
readiness and instantaneousness in changing from one degree
of tension to another, which electricity itself hardly surpasses.
Slight turning of the hand may be permitted when the thumb
cannot otherwise reach its key. This turning must be studied
as a separate motion, and should occur immediately after
item No. 10, in Complete Analysis of Mechanism of the
Scale. It is to be regarded as an expedient for facilitating
other movements, and should be employed only for a few
weeks or months. For this reason it is not included in the
analysis of the mechanism of the scale. After thorough
acquaintance with the necessary finger locations, and after
the formation of correct habits in retaining them, turning
the hand may be discarded.

It is true that some persons never become able to dispense wholly with this turning of the hand. But the necessity for it will be obviated in many cases by gathering the fingers together by sidewise movements as follows: In the first section of the scale, after the third finger has struck, the second finger may be moved sidewise, fairly touching the third and as close to it as possible. It will then be perceived that the thumb can reach under the hand to its required key with much greater ease. In the second section of the scale, after the third finger has struck, the second may be moved to the closest proximity; and after the fourth has struck, the third and second may be moved close as possible to the fourth.

PASSING THE THUMB.

Rigid discipline in passing the thumb depends primarily on exactness of control and motion, but also, secondarily, on suppleness in the joint where the thumb is connected with the hand close to the wrist. Additional suppleness in this joint may be gained by firmly bending the third section of the thumb (that nearest the hand) back and under the hand, repeating this exercise from ten to fifty times a day for some weeks. *Much care is necessary in order to avoid straining the muscles or tendons in all such manipulation.* The first feeling of over-exertion, which the sensitive nerves always impart, and which feeling must always instantly be yielded to, should cause one to refrain from further exercise until the muscles are perfectly rested.

THE LEGATO TOUCH.

All scales and all finger passages must become absolutely perfect as regards connection of tones. The legato touch depends on the retaining of each tone until producing the next, so that tone shall meet tone, and yet they shall not blend one with the other. (Any blending produces what is called the Legatissimo touch.) The hearing and judgment must combine to instruct the will in the production of the legato touch.

The practice of the scales should be conducted as follows :

THE OUTLINE OR SCHEME FOR PRACTICE
EXERCISE 1.—RIGHT HAND.

Practice of first and second Elements of Mechanism (finger action and passing of thumb.) First series of keys ascending. Fingers used, 1, 2, 3, pass thumb.

EXERCISE 2.—LEFT HAND.
The same, descending.

EXERCISE 3.—RIGHT HAND.

First, second, and first elements. Finger action, passing of thumb, and action of thumb under hand. Fingers used, 1, 2, 3, 1. First series of keys ascending, and one of second series. (This exercise of striking with thumb under the hand should often receive separate attention.)

EXERCISE 4.—LEFT HAND.
The same, descending.

EXERCISE 5.—RIGHT HAND.

First, second, and third elements. Finger action, passing of thumb and transfer of fingers, hand, and arm. Fingers used, 1, 2, 3, 1, *and transfer.* First series of keys and one of second series.

EXERCISE 6.—LEFT HAND.
The same, descending.

EXERCISE 7.—RIGHT HAND.

Practice of transfer alone, the thumb holding its key and the hand moving over it.

EXERCISE 8.—LEFT HAND.
The same, descending.

EXERCISE 9.—RIGHT HAND.

First, second, third, and first elements. Fingers used, 1, 2, 3, 1, 2. The return of the finger action after the transfer, which is the object of the exercise, must be very accurate. Especial care of position is necessary after the transfer.

EXERCISE 10.—LEFT HAND.

The same, descending.

EXERCISE 11.—RIGHT HAND.

Second series of keys. First and second elements of mechanism. 1, 2, 3, 4, pass thumb.

EXERCISE 12.—LEFT HAND.

The same, descending.

EXERCISE 13.—RIGHT HAND.

Second series of keys, and one of first series in the next octave above. First, second, and first elements of mechanism. Fingers used, 1, 2, 3, 4, 1.

EXERCISE 14.—LEFT HAND.

The same, descending.

EXERCISE 15.—RIGHT HAND.

First, second, and third elements. Fingers used, 1, 2, 3, 4, 1. The thumb should be exercised by itself under the hand.

EXERCISE 16.—LEFT HAND.

The same, descending.

EXERCISE 17.—RIGHT HAND.

Practice of transfer alone, thumb holding its key.

EXERCISE 18.—LEFT HAND.

The same.

EXERCISE 19.—RIGHT HAND.

First, second, third, and first elements. Fingers used, 1, 2, 3, 4, 1, 2. The finger action after the transfer must be well individualized.

EXERCISE 20.—LEFT HAND.

The same, descending.

EXERCISES 21-40.

Should comprise the reverse movements in reverse directions of the scale with separate hands as above.

EXERCISE 41.—RIGHT HAND.

Complete scale, one octave and one note.

EXERCISE 42.—LEFT HAND.

The same.

EXERCISE 43.—RIGHT HAND.

Complete scale, two octaves and one note.

EXERCISE 44.—LEFT HAND.

The same.

EXERCISE 45.—RIGHT HAND.

The same in reverse direction ; *i. e.*, ascending instead of descending.

EXERCISE 46.—LEFT HAND.

The same in reverse direction ; *i. e.*, ascending instead of descending.

EXERCISE 47.—RIGHT HAND.

Scale in four octaves, ascending and descending.

EXERCISE 48.—LEFT HAND.

The same.

EXERCISES 49-54.

Scale (each hand separately) *p. mf.* and *f.* The fortissimo touch is not safe for most pupils at all before the second stage of practice.

EXERCISES 55-62.

Scale (each hand separately) in different degrees of fluency from $\mathbf{f} = 60$ to $\mathbf{f} = 104$ (or less), allowing two notes of the scale to each count or beat, each to be represented by an eighth note.

EXERCISE 63.

Scale with two hands.

EXERCISE 64.

Scale with two hands in contrary motion.

EXERCISE 65.

Scale with two hands in sixths.

EXERCISE 66.

Same as 65 in tenths.

EXERCISE 67.

Same as 65 in thirds.

It is not, of course, necessary that the preceding plan be carried out in all the scales. If carried out in the scale of C Major and A Minor that would usually prove enough to establish correct habits. More practice than this is however, necessary for some students. The scale cannot be studied too thoroughly. All Major and Minor scales should be practiced in this stage, the Minor scales in the Melodic form as in Plaidy.

CHORDS AND ARPEGGIOS.

THEORY AND PRACTICE OF CHORDS.

THEORY OF CHORDS.

The theory of the structure of chords should be presented and fully elucidated, as in the study of harmony,* before the practice of chords is undertaken.

---

* See Richter's Manual of Harmony, published by Schirmer, N. Y. (Palmer's Theory of Music, published by Ditson, N. Y. and Boston, is to be commended for its clearness of explanation, but is not as good an authority as Richter.)

FINGERING OF CHORDS.

To this point the fingers have occupied only adjacent keys. In playing the chord C E G with the right hand the same finger locations may be employed and the finger application then is $\frac{5}{3}$. This fingering is usually most suitable when the hand is not obliged to change its location quickly or frequently in passing to or from the chord. In other cases the fingering may be $\frac{4}{2}$, thus affording a more open position of the hand; and $\frac{3}{1}$ may also be used where the connections require it, but less frequently than the others.

POISE OF UNEMPLOYED FINGERS.

In case $\frac{4}{2}$ is used, the fifth finger should be poised over the middle of the key A, just touching the key without pressing it down, when the finger action is used. The third finger is poised over the key F in like manner. When the fingering $\frac{3}{2}$ is chosen, the fourth and fifth fingers should be poised over the middle of the keys A and B. The habit of an accurate adjustment of unemployed fingers is an important one, and cannot be too earnestly cultivated. The finger applications, and the poise of unemployed fingers of the left hand, should correspond with those of the right hand. The chords E G C and G C D are to be studied as above.

TWO KINDS OF PRACTICE NEEDED.

As these chords (C E G, E G C, and G C E,) are played in different ways they demand at least two kinds of practice. They may be practiced with finger action and hand action.

REQUISITES OF FINGER ACTION IN CHORD PLAYING.

Finger action in chord playing demands great independence. It demands also greater tension than simple five note figures in the muscles of the arm by which the hand and arm are supported and steadied. In the fingering $\begin{smallmatrix} 3 \\ 2 \\ 1 \end{smallmatrix}$, *some* hands will need especial discipline (perhaps by means of manipulation by the teacher and by the pupil himself) as the ligament binding the third section of the second and third fingers does not always possess sufficient suppleness to maintain its power of extension without careful stretching. Manipulation is a useful, but not the only means of securing this power of extension, for many hands profit equally by holding the keys for several seconds, *accurate relationships of all parts being established.* This should be followed by a complete relaxation of the muscles and nerves when the hand leaves the keyboard. This power of extension is an essential requisite of finger action in chord playing.

THE PRACTICE.

• Finger action in chord playing cannot always be perfected at this stage, and little more than an illustration of it should be attempted here. A week's effective practice would usually be sufficient, if it is resumed at a later stage in the course.

THE FINGER ACTION IN PRACTICE.

The first practice should be undertaken with a very light and delicate, yet unyielding touch, that the strength of the finger alone may be used. After two or three days of this practice with reference to perfecting the power of extension by the process above suggested, and perfecting the finger action, especial attention should be given to the balance or proportion of tone.

ARTISTIC PRODUCTION OF THE CHORD.—THE TONE.

The highest tone in a chord given by the right hand, supposing it to be a tone of the melody, should be a little stronger than the others in almost all cases. Great care should be taken not to fatigue the hand in this practice. To exhaust it is frequently to ruin it. Strength should be first gained by use, later by exertion, as the muscles and nerves gain in development sufficiently to render it safe.

ARTICULATION, DURATION, AND TERMINATION.

The chord should have a definite point of articulation, a definite period of duration, and a definite point of termination. Exact simultaneousness in the production of all the tones, is a vital condition of the chord-effect. The sense of perfectness must be satisfied in all the above-mentioned details of the artistic production.

Let the teacher prescribe the amount of time or the number of repetitions to be given to practice to each of the above-mentioned elements, as he should do in all technical exercises. At least twenty-five repetitions per day ought to be prescribed.

HAND ACTION IN CHORD PLAYING.

The action of the hand in chord playing should be studied as methodically as the finger action in scale playing. This has in its fundamental technical exercise three elements, viz.; the Upward Motion, the Point of Repose in Space, and the Downward Motion. An accurate position or relationship of the various parts, should be preserved at every point.

REQUISITES OF HAND ACTION.

The mechanical requisites of hand action are four in number: Unity or Singleness, Directness, Steadiness, and Impulsiveness. In other words, the hand should move without disturbing the arm or the fingers, the fingers being held with a tension sufficient to insure their quietness. The hand should move *directly* from or toward the precise location, steadily, and yet with an impulse sufficiently positive to produce the tone desired.

The tension of the nerves and muscles controlling the fingers, should be somewhat greater here than in previous exercises, but no more than is necessary for securing independence, unity, and steadiness of motion, and the poise of unemployed fingers. The exact adaptation of the tension can only be determined by judgment and experience. (See " Tension," page 16.)

The fingers being adjusted to the keys, in accordance with directions on page 21, those which are not to be employed in striking should be raised and kept elevated from a quarter to half an inch above the level of those which are to strike, thus establishing the poise necessary to prevent them from striking with the others. In maintaining the poise, care should be exercised that it shall not occasion false tension, or an undue contraction of the muscles.

APPLICATION OF FORCE.

The force employed should be medium at first, unless the touch proves to be weak and nerveless. Let nerve force, especially (*i. e.*, of the motor nerves), and not muscular force be sought for as a rule at first, and after three days of practice, muscular power, little by little.

In developing the hand action, the elements may be reduced to two, allowing not a moment of interruption or repose between the upward and downward motions, thus affording the artistic blending of the motions referred to in the " Practice of the Scale," and securing perfect elasticity. The looseness of the wrist and complete passivity of the parts near it, must be as great as when the hand drops from the arm in falling asleep.

AUXILIARY MOTIONS IN CHORD PLAYING.

Auxiliary motions are necessary, *First*, In passing from one chord to another in the use of white keys only; *Second*, In passing from a chord containing only white keys to one containing one or more black keys, or passing *vice versa.*

Auxiliary motions of the first class consist in a sidewise motion of the hand and arm toward the right or left, as the case may require. Those of the second class consist in forward or backward motions, toward or from the black keys, as the case may require. This kind usually involves, also, some sidewise motion. Elasticity of the motion of the upper arm as well as the fore-arm, must, in both cases, be carefully cultivated.

Practice of these mere *motions* of the hand and arm is desirable, even if only a few moments be given to it daily. It may then be combined with hand action in chord playing, using the chords E, G, C, and F, A, D, in alternation (with both fingerings) for illustration of the first class; and G, B, E, and A, C, F#, for illustration of the second class (in this case also using both fingerings).

FIRST CLASS.   SECOND CLASS.

The backward and forward motion is not *always* necessary when black keys are met with. If the black keys occur frequently, the hand should be kept closer in the range of the black keys than usual (*i. e.*, nearer to the name-board), thus obviating all necessity for frequent backward and forward motion.

ARPEGGIOS OR ARPEGGII.

DEFINITION.—An arpeggio is a series of tones which constitute a chord taken successively instead of simultaneously, and extended through any desired number of octaves.

THEORY OF FINGERING.

The fingering of arpeggios is derived from that of chords.

The arpeggio, $\overline{C}, \overline{E}, \overline{G}, \overline{\overline{C}}, \overline{\overline{E}}, \overline{\overline{G}}, \overline{\overline{\overline{C}}},$* derives its fingering for the right hand from the third fingering of the chord $\overline{C}, \overline{E}, \overline{G}, \left\{ \begin{matrix} 3 \\ 2 \\ 1 \end{matrix} \right\}$ each octave of the arpeggio being a repetition of the one before it. Its fingering for the left hand is derived from the second fingering of the chord E, G, $\overline{C}, \left\{ \begin{matrix} 1 \\ 2 \\ 4 \end{matrix} \right\}$ the first key C being taken, exceptionally, with the fifth finger, and each octave thereafter being a repetition of the first.

The fingerings which are usually employed are, in many cases, very defective, as they do not easily admit of perfect connections of tone. For example, the usual fingering for the left hand in the arpeggio D, F♯, A, $\overline{D}, \overline{F}♯, \overline{A}, \overline{\overline{D}},$ is 5, 4, 2, 1, 4, 2, 1, but it should be 5, *3*, 2, 1, 3, 2, 1, thus affording greater ease of connection in passing the fingers over in ascending, or the thumb under in descending. For all fingerings of the common chord arpeggios, see arpeggios with fingerings prepared in accordance with the principles above suggested, and which accompany this Outline.

Arpeggio passages requiring the greatest velocity, should be fingered with the use of the fourth finger (in the above-mentioned forms and those corresponding), instead of the third, as that affords a more natural relationship, and consequently greater facility of motion. This should be employed only where the pure legato effect may with propriety be sacrificed to the velocity.

The principles of mechanical action and the elements of mechanism, are, with a few exceptions, the same in arpeggio as in scale playing. (See "Elements and Analysis of

---

* $\overline{C}$ indicates "middle C"; $\overline{\overline{C}}$ indicates the octave above "middle C"; $\overline{\overline{\overline{C}}}$ two octaves above "middle C."

Mechanism of the Scale," page 31, and apply the same in all practicable details of arpeggio practice in slow movement.)

EXCEPTIONS.

The first exception relates to the fingering, and is mentioned above. The *scale* has an *established* fingering; the arpeggio fingering may frequently change on the above-mentioned principles.

The connection of tone in a legato scale, must always be effected by an accurate and sufficient retention of each tone with the finger; in the arpeggio, on the other hand, the connection may sometimes, though not at all frequently, be effected by the use of the pedal. The use of the pedal is subject to the laws of tone and expression. This topic will be treated in a work which is in preparation embracing tone, expression, phrasing, and general interpretation.

The third exception to be named, is the omission of the second element of mechanism (the passing of the thumb), which occurs when the greatest velocity and facility are needed. With some hands, all these exceptions must occur more frequently than is above suggested, but usually at a considerable disadvantage to the artistic result.

THE APPLICATION OF THE SECOND ELEMENT OF MECH-
ANISM IN ARPEGGIO PRACTICE.

The finger action is subject to the same conditions as in scale a playing, but a somewhat greater tension in the muscles of the arm is required, to insure perfect quietness of the hand. Therefore, we may pass at once to the second element of mechanism, the passing of the thumb.

REGULATION AS TO DIRECTION OF MOTION.

The regulation as to direction of motion, is precisely the same as in the scale. The regulation as to time of motion, is made on *the same principle* as in the scale, but the principle has a different application. Immediately after the second finger has taken its key, the thumb should be carried under the hand for its first stage of motion to that key which forms the interval of the fifth with the first one. For example, in the right hand part of the first form of the common chord arpeggio of C, the thumb in its first stage of motion passes from the key $\overline{C}$ to the key $\overline{G}$. For its second stage of motion it should pass immediately after the third finger has taken its key, to the octave, that is, the key $\overline{\overline{C}}$.

FIRST AUXILIARY MOTION.

Some turning of the hand to a line oblique to the keys is usually necessary. This should be effected between the first and second stages of passing the thumb. As little turning of the hand as possible should be employed, for the reason that in fluent or somewhat rapid movements, the motions become too complicated to be well conducted. The necessity for it is greatly reduced by discipline in reaching under the hand with the thumb, in such a manner that the hand-joint and surrounding muscles are made to increase their capacity of extension, and to yield with suppleness to the stretching of the thumb. Some manipulation is also beneficial. Each finger after it leaves its key, may be carried by impulsive lateral motion to the closest position to the next finger, thus rendering the passing of the thumb much easier for many persons.

EXEMPLIFICATION OF FINGER ACTION.
FIRST PAIR OF EXERCISES.

The practice of the arpeggio should begin with an exercise $\left(\begin{array}{cccccccc} \overline{C}, & \overline{E}, & \overline{G}, & \overline{E}, & \overline{C}, & \overline{E}, & \overline{G}, & \overline{E}, \\ 1 & 2 & 3 & 2 & 1 & 2 & 3 & 2 \end{array} \right)$ for the exemplification of the first element, the finger action.

All tension which will prove necessary in the arpeggio itself, should here be employed. The application of force may be very slight. The tone should be pure and musical,

and the sense of excellence in tone must be well satisfied as
in all arpeggios and all other practice.   With left hand the

exercise is $\begin{smallmatrix} G, & E, & C, & E, & G, & E, & C, & E. \\ 1 & 2 & 3 & 2 & 1 & 2 & 3 & 2 \end{smallmatrix}$

This exercise may be practiced after the twentieth or fif-
tieth repetition with some fluency.   Corresponding exercises
may introduce other forms of arpeggios.

SECOND PAIR OF EXERCISES.

$\begin{smallmatrix} \overline{C}, & \overline{E}, & \overline{G}, & \overline{E}, & \overline{C}, & \overline{E}, & \overline{G}, & \overline{E}. \\ 1 & 2 & 3 & 2 & 1 & 2 & 3 & 2 \end{smallmatrix}$ | $\begin{smallmatrix} \overline{G}, & E, & C, & E, & G, & E, & C, & E. \\ 1 & 2 & 3 & 2 & 1 & 2 & 3 & 2 \end{smallmatrix}$

RIGHT HAND.   LEFT HAND.

This is to be accompanied by the passing of the thumb,
first and second stages of motion, and turning of the hand,
the latter between the first and second stages of motion of
the thumb.   Only *one motion at a time* should be used in the
first practice of all exercises.   The thumb must be carried
fully to the octave in the second stage.   This exercise must
be practiced *very slowly*, giving from two to four seconds to
each tone.

THIRD PAIR OF EXERCISES.

Right hand, $\begin{smallmatrix} \overline{G}, & \overline{\overline{C}}, & \overline{G}, & \overline{\overline{C}}. \\ 3 & 1 & 3 & 1 \end{smallmatrix}$ Left hand, $\begin{smallmatrix} \overline{C}, & G, & \overline{C}, & G. \\ 3 & 1 & 3 & 1 \end{smallmatrix}$ The
position should be taken with the thumb and third finger,
both over the key $\overline{G}$ (right hand), or $\overline{C}$ (left hand), the unemployed fingers at the same time taking their proper loca-
tions,* and the correct form of the hand being assumed and
maintained.   Then follows—

1. Striking the key (third finger). The third finger should
hold the key firmly, that the following action of the thumb
may not detract from the connection of the tones.

2. Turning the hand.

---

* Without this attention to unemployed fingers they usually assume some false
tension.

3. Passing the thumb.
4. Striking with thumb.
5. Striking third finger.
6. Return of thumb.
7. Turning hand back.

It will be observed that a complete analysis of the mechanism is not here undertaken, the pressure, the release of the key, points of repose, etc., not being specified. The teacher should draft one for reference and for his own guidance, as also the complete analysis of mechanism of the entire arpeggio. All such analyses are of value to the teacher as well as to the pupil.

FOURTH PAIR OF EXERCISES.

$\overline{G}, \overline{\overline{C}}, \overline{\overline{E}}, \overline{\overline{C}}, \overline{G}, \overline{\overline{C}}, \overline{\overline{E}}, \overline{\overline{C}}.$	$\overline{C}, G, E, G, \overline{C}, G, E, G.$
3 1 2 1 3 1 2 1	3 1 2 1 3 1 2 1
RIGHT HAND.	LEFT HAND.

In addition to the mechanical elements of the preceding exercises, we have here the transfer of fingers, hand and arm. This should be so effected as to open the hand fully, and to admit the precise application of the second and third fingers to the keys $\overline{\overline{E}}$ and G (right hand), and E and C (left hand). The motions should be well individualized, *i. e.*, only one motion at a time should be attempted.

FIFTH PAIR OF EXERCISES.

Right hand, complete arpeggio, ascending. Left hand, complete arpeggio, descending. From two to five seconds should be allowed for each tone.

SIXTH PAIR OF EXERCISES.

Right hand, complete arpeggio, descending. Left hand, complete arpeggio, ascending.

SEVENTH PAIR OF EXERCISES.

Right hand, throughout, ascending and descending. Left hand, the same. (Group in couplets and quartolets.)

EIGHTH PAIR OF EXERCISES.

Right hand and left hand together. The same together, contrary motion.

NINTH PAIR OF EXERCISES.

Right hand fifteen times piano, and fifteen times forte. Left hand, the same.

TENTH PAIR OF EXERCISES.

Right hand, triplets. Left hand, triplets.

It will be observed that to this point the arpeggio has been played without accent, other than that of couplets and quartolets. Other forms may here be introduced, but perfect connection of tone must be preserved, not allowing the ear to be deceived in the smallest degree. *Perfect evenness* of succession is indispensable.

ELEVENTH PAIR OF EXERCISES.

Right hand, groups of five. Left hand, groups of five.

Other groups may be practiced in the reviews, as groups six, seven, eight, and nine notes.

THE SEXTOLETS.

The Sextolet is sometimes employed as a triple couplet, and sometimes as a double triplet. These subdivisions should not be usually suggested, however, by any accent, even though a weak accent. They are often evident by the connection in which these groups occur, or by some accompanying part.

Moderate velocity only should be sought for at this stage. Arpeggios should be reviewed for the attainment of greater velocity, power, etc., after the practice of—

1. The moving figures of Plaidy's Technical Studies, and all necessary transpositions of the same.

2. The first review of the scales.

3. The First Book (or half of it) of Tausig's Daily

Studies (published by Schirmer, price $2). It is a very useful set of exercises.

4. The chromatic scale.

MOVING FIGURES.

These exercises embrace the same elements as the scale, but usually exemplified in less extended motions.

1. Finger action.
2. Passing of thumb,
3. Transfer of fingers, hand, and arm.

In many figures the transfer required is only for the distance of an inch—the distance from key to key. In such figures a just appreciation and perception of the necessary distance of motion must be insured.

TRANSPOSITIONS.

It is desirable to transpose some of these figures into other keys than C. In practicing in other keys, great precision should be exercised in adapting and adjusting the fingers to their successive locations. In each location, at least two fingers should be adjusted to their keys before proceeding to carry out the figure. Analyses of locations and changes are to be made in preparing for the practice by study.

From one to four months will be required for the practice of the moving figures here mentioned.

FIRST REVIEW OF THE SCALES.

This review constitutes the second stage of practice, and should be conducted on the same general principles as the practice of the first stage. Each day's practice should begin by allowing one second at least to each tone. The rapidity may be gradually increased through the hour devoted to them. After a few days, a higher degree of velocity may be attempted. As successive scales are taken, the velocity may be still further increased. Due care should be exercised,

however, that these efforts for velocity never carry one be-
yond the point where a sufficient individualization of the
motions is preserved.

In this stage of the practice the harmonic form of the
minor scales may be practiced.   In this form due care must
be exercised that the sixth and seventh keys in each octave
are properly prepared for, by means of an accurate transfer
and adjustment of the fingers.   In rapid movements, this
preparation should be very promptly made.

As rapidity is attempted, the amount of finger motion
must usually be reduced.

From two to four months should generally be allowed for
this review.   Mere *familiarity* with the scale requires little
time, but the *attainment* of SKILL in playing, must, of necessity, consume much time, which yields, however, a splendid
return.

TAUSIG'S DAILY STUDIES.   (MOVING FIGURES.)

In these exercises the thumb comes upon black keys so
often that many awkward and unnecessary movements result,
unless the practice is rightly conducted.   They may be
avoided by keeping the thumb always in range of the black
keys, and the fingers in their exact form and relationships.

The first exercises require a very close setting of the fingers, as the chromatic figures of which they are composed
require that the fingers shall be very near together.   The
necessary directness of the finger action should here be carefully observed.

Other elements of mechanism are as in simple moving figures and in the scales.

THE CHROMATIC SCALE.

The chromatic scale may here be introduced.   It should
be noticed that partial transfers only are made as in moving
figures, and not complete transfers, as in the scale.   Two fingerings only need be used.

FIRST REVIEW OF ARPEGGIOS.

❧ This should be conducted on the same general principles as the first review of the scales.

REPEATED NOTES.

It is necessary to devote very little time to this class of exercises, say from two to three weeks. They may be introduced earlier than at this point, if found convenient, but never until after the first practice of the scales.

· HOLDING-NOTE EXERCISES.

Five-note exercises with holding notes may be introduced here, or in connection with the first review of the scales. They should *always* be practiced concurrently with arpeggios. For comment on their use, see page 28.

Usually but little time should be devoted to them. Fifteen minutes daily, from two to four weeks, is sufficient.

ARPEGGIO MOVING FIGURES.

Moving figures derived from arpeggios may next be introduced. The principles of their mechanism are the same as in moving figures and Tausig's Daily Studies. They require no especial attention in this Outline. The connections of tone are sometimes effected with difficulty, and are frequently deceptive to a careless ear. The principles of their fingerings are based mainly on those of the arpeggios. They must be investigated and specified in a corresponding manner by the teacher.

DOMINANT SEVENTH ARPEGGIOS.

These are treated in a manner similar to the arpeggios of the common chord. They afford most excellent discipline in finger action. They require a strong tension without any false contraction of nerves and muscles of the arm, and a very supple hand, without loss of precision in the relationships of the various parts of the hand. The teacher should write out the analysis of the mechanism, and construct formulas for the practice of these exercises on the preceding models. They are to be fingered on the principles exemplified in common chord arpeggios. They should be practiced in all keys.

OCTAVES.

These may be practiced after dominant seventh arpeggios, and usually in the third year. What has been said concerning chords will generally apply to octaves. But it should be observed that the subject of chord playing was developed in the preceding pages only as that particular part of the subject required. The playing of octaves, and chords with the octaves, requires in the various circumstances three kinds of movements:—

1. Action of the fingers for legato playing.

2. Action of hand, in detached tones, with the lesser degrees of force.

3. Action of forearm, in detached tones, in greater degrees of force and in distant movements.

Movements of the whole arm are often required in bravura playing, and in *all cases where sudden changes to distant keys occur.* Immediately after the attack of the tones, the muscles should be relaxed to the lowest degree of tension consistent with the retention of the tone. When the hand and wrist have attained suppleness, the tension may be increased instead of reduced, while holding the key.

Considerable effort is needed to maintain the necessary extension, unless the hand is quite large or extremely elastic. The muscles must be firmly controlled for this purpose.

"Kullak's Octave School," is quite a satisfactory guide, both theoretical and practical, in the practice of full chords and octaves. Part II is published by Schirmer, of New York, at $2.50. Part III is not needed by some students, as it consists of selections of works in very general use.

DOUBLE NOTE EXERCISES AND SCALES.

" Double notes " require in their less extended and less fluent successions *double tone connections, i. e.*, connections in the upper and lower series of tones. This is comparatively easy in thirds and fourths, as it is simply the act of retaining one tone until the next is produced, with perfectly natural rela tionships of the fingers. But in sixths the proper extension of the fingers and hand usually causes some difficulty, and requires especial care, as regards form of the hand and connection of tones.

When three or more double tones are used in succession, either the upper or lower series of tones must lose somewhat of their connectedness. The part in which this slight disconnection may take place, should be determined in advance by the teacher or player. Such cases occur, of course, where the thumb or any finger must be used twice in succession.

Scales in double tones may be fingered as in Plaidy's Technical Studies. The fingering of the scale of C given below is, however, preferable to that given by Plaidy.

ELEMENTS OF MECHANISM.

In addition to some elements specified in simple scale practice, and which need not here be mentioned, we have the following:—

1. Extension and contraction of fingers and hand.

2. (Exceptional.) Premature release of key for disconnection.

The following diagram will show the principles of the best method of fingering, and the points where the premature release of the key, and the consequent disconnection occurs:—

In the descending passage all the disconnections occur in the upper series of tones.

The scales may also be practiced demi-legato, demi-staccato, and staccato, with the action of the hand. In the two former cases the downward motion is principal, the upward motion is incidental. In the latter they are reversed. (See pages 40, 41.)

TRILLS.

A good school for the trill may be formed found in Lebert and. Stark's Piano Method, Part III. This is an excellent method, and indeed almost the only one worthy of general use.

The element of pressure or weight in the touch required in the trill, is reduced to a minimum when rapidity is demanded.

Until the trill is perfectly understood, and has also been many times perfectly performed, *it should be practiced only from explicitly written groups of notes*, in order that no habit of indefiniteness in performance shall be contracted. All trills should be practiced with a definite number of notes for each count or fraction of a count, until fluency is attained. The number of tones for each count should be prescribed by the teacher or decided on by the student, before beginning the practice.   Groups of two, four, or six should be played to each count, according as the counts are short or long.   The practice should be slow for the first ten repetitions, and may be increased in quickness, by using more tones, playing groups of four, six, or eight, instead of two, four, or six.

The teemination of the trill should be in strictly diatonic or chromatic conjunct successions of tones. All disjunct successions (*i. e.*, successions by skips) should be avoided.

The treminal group of tones should conform to the melodic connection, and will consist sometimes of four and sometimes of five tones. In both cases perfect evenness in succession, equality and in tone are essential. The triplet terminal group, though used by some composers, is usually inelegant.

Facility in playing the trill may be developed in the use of a very slow movement with great impulsiveness of each motion, a minimum pressure, and perfect quietness of hand. All the principles specified in " Two-Note Exercises " must here receive their most precise application.

APPLICATION OF LAWS OF MECHANISM IN ETUDES AND
OTHER COMPOSITIONS.

In the practice of etudes and pieces of every description, the details of mechanism, including the fingerings, the finger locations, and transfers, the positions, the tensions, the motions, the applications of force, and all other items, should each receive separate and careful attention, and each be thoroughly practiced.

In finishing a piece or etude, and while devoting one's attention to the interpretation (the tone, accent, phrasing, contrast, shading, movement, form, design, etc.), the attention to mechanism should be subordinated to these other matters. Practice for uniting a technical with a musical element is, however, indispensable. It may very safely be subordinated, for with the thorough practice of Technique which precedes the study of interpretation, the nerves, muscles, and members have attained a power of automatic action, and employ their correct forces, relationships, and motions from a power of habit, or from an acquired sense of fitness and convenience.

In inspired interpretation the thought of Technique no longer exists. The science of mechanism has served its purpose, and has been annihilated.

THE TECHNIQUE OF LOCATIONS AND TRANSFERS.

The study of Locations and Transfers is of very great importance in connecting the elements of Technique with practical performance. Without this study, confusion often

arises in regard to the order, and also in regard to the kinds
of motions which are necessary.

Locations are given places on the key-board to which the
fingers are applied. For example, the thumb of the right
hand may be placed on *c* and other fingers on each succeeding white key in natural relationship. This is a five-key
location, *i. e.*, a placing of the fingers, which covers five keys
of the scale of C.

Another example: The thumb of the right hand may be
placed on *c*, the second finger on *e* and other fingers following on succeeding white keys in natural relationship. This
is a six-key location, *i. e.*, a placing of the fingers, which
covers six keys of the scale of C.

Another example: The thumb of the right hand may be
placed on $d_\sharp$, the second finger on $g_\sharp$, the third on $a_\sharp$, the
fourth on *b*, and the fifth on $c_\sharp$. This is a seven-key location,
as the fingers then cover seven keys of the scale of $g_\sharp$ minor.

Locations may be thus classified :—

1. Locations in natural relationship of fingers.
2. Locations in contracted relationship of fingers.
3. Locations in extended relationship of fingers.
4. Locations in inverted relationship of fingers.

They may also be classified as:—

1. Locations of white keys.
2. Locations of black keys.
3. Locations of partly white and partly black keys.

Locations on white keys are of course on a lower level
than those of black keys. The fingers, hand and arm, all,
must therefore be at a slightly greater height on black keys
than on white. This difference will be merely a difference
of height between black and white keys.

When the fingers are all on the same level, the finger
action is uniformly the same in amount in taking all keys.
When, however, the fingers are partly on white and partly on

black keys, a little confusion of mind often arises concerning
the equality of motion. Each finger should rise an equal
distance from each key, whether it be white or black. For
example, if a finger rises half an inch from a white key it
should also rise half an inch from a black. This refers to the
preparatory upward motion in elementary practice. Different
parts of the hand itself should also conform to the different
heights of the key levels. This last requirement may be a
difficult one, and perhaps in some cases impracticable, if the
hand is not quite supple.

TRANSFERS.

Transfers are lateral or sidewise motions from one location to another.

They are thus classified:—

1. Transfers of fingers.
2. Transfers of fingers and hand.
3. Transfers of fingers, hand and arm.

The second is used rather infrequently. The third kind
is to be used most of all. Some lateral motion of the upper
arm as well as of the fore-arm is necessary in all passage-
playing and in certain kinds of figure-playing.

Transfers are also classified as:—

1. Partial.
2. Partially complete, and—
3. Complete.

They are *partial* when a part of the fingers move to different keys while some of them retain their keys without
moving away from them.

EXAMPLE.

PARTIAL TRANSFER.

They are *partially* complete transfers, when all the fingers
are carried to different keys from those which they were indi-
vidually using, but some of the keys are still retained although
by different fingers.

EXAMPLE.

PARTIALLY COMPLETE TRANSFER.

They are complete when all fingers are moved to entirely
different keys, none of those preceding being retained.
They may be either connected or disconnected.

EXAMPLES.

COMPLETE CONNECTED TRANSFER.   COMPLETE DISCONNECTED TRANSFER.

It will be observed that the partial and partially complete
transfers are made by, first, a transfer of one finger (the
thumb in the above examples), and then of the remaining
fingers, and in many cases of the fore-arm or whole arm.

In the example of the partial transfer, the first finger
(thumb) only is moved in the beginning of the change, and
immediately afterward the second moves to its new location.

In the example of the partially complete transfer, the
thumb moves first, then afterward the remaining fingers are
moved to their respective places. This is the manner of
transfers to be adopted in Plaidy's and Tausig's moving
figures. The hand and fore-arm both participate in the
second part of the change, and the upper arm also if following groups continue to ascend or descend.

In the example of the complete connected transfer, when
the thumb reaches down to *c*, the hand, arm and all the

fingers except the fifth should move toward the body for the first part of the change, the second, third and fourth fingers moving only a part of the distance toward their new location and partially straightening themselves. After the thumb has taken its key, and while still holding it, all the fingers, including the fifth, are moved to their new places, and the new location is then entirely assumed.

In the following figures unemployed fingers must have definite places, and the locations are locations of five keys although in each case a smaller number of keys is used.

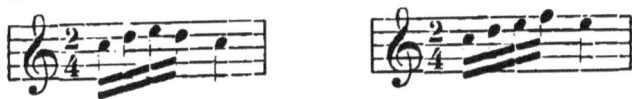

It is only with inverted relationship of fingers that a four or three key location is possible.

EXAMPLES.

THREE KEY LOCATION.   FOUR KEY LOCATION.

It will be observed that these narrow limits are reached by contraction, as six or seven key locations are reached by extension.

The study of Locations and Transfers in connection with the practice of Etudes is of great importance.

FINGERING OF MAJOR SCALES.

Scale Names.	
C, G, D, A, & E.	R. H.—1, 2, 3, 1, 2, 3, 4, 1, 2; 3, 1, 2, 3, 4, 5. L. H.—5, 4, 3, 2, 1, 3, 2, 1, 4, 3, 2, 1, 3, 2; 1.
B & C♭.	R. H.—1, 2, 3, 1, 2, 3, 4, 1, 2, 3, 1, 2, 3, 4, 5. L. H.—4, 3, 2, 1, 4, 3, 2, 1, 3, 2, 1, 4, 3, 2, 1.
C♯ & D♭.	R. H.—2, 3, 1, 2, 3, 4, 1, 2, 3, 1, 2, 3, 4, 1, 2. L. H.—3, 2, 1, 4, 3, 2, 1, 3, 2, 1, 4, 3, 2, 1, 2,
A♭.	R. H.—2, 3, 1, 2, 3, 1, 2, 3, 4, 1, 2, 3, 1, 2, 3. L. H.—3, 2, 1, 4, 3, 2, 1, 3, 2, 1, 4, 3, 2, 1, 2.
E♭.	R. H.—2, 1, 2, 3, 4, 1, 2, 3, 1, 2, 3, 4, 1, 2, 3. L. H.—3, 2, 1, 4, 3, 2, 1, 3, 2, 1, 4, 3, 2, 1, 2.
G♭ & F♯.	R. H.—2, 3, 4, 1, 2, 3, 1, 2, 3, 4, 1, 2, 3, 4, 5. L. H.—4, 3, 2, 1, 3, 2, 1, 4, 3, 2, 1, 3, 2, 1, 2.
F.	R. H.—1, 2, 3, 4, 1, 2, 3, 1, 2, 3, 4, 1, 2, 3, 4. L. H.—5, 4, 3, 2, 1, 3, 2, 1, 4, 3, 2, 1, 3, 2, 1.
B♭.	R. H.—2, 1, 2, 3, 1, 2, 3, 4, 1, 2, 3, 1, 2, 3, 4. L. H.—3, 2, 1, 4, 3, 2, 1, 3, 2, 1, 4, 3, 2, 1, 3.

FINGERING OF MINOR SCALES, ASCENDING.*

Scale Names.	
A, E, C, G, & D.	R. H.—1, 2, 3, 1, 2, 3, 4, 1, 2, 3, 1, 2, 3, 4, 5. L. H.—5, 4, 3, 2, 1, 3, 2, 1, 4, 3, 2, 1, 3, 2, 1.
B.	R. H.—1, 2, 3, 1, 2, 3, 4, 1, 2, 3, 1, 2, 3, 4, 5. L. H.—4, 4, 2, 1, 4, 3, 2, 1, 3, 2, 1, 4, 3, 2, 1.
F#.	R. H.—2, 3, 1, 2, 3, 4, 1, 2, 3, 1, 2, 3, 4, 1, 3. L. H.—4, 3, 2, 1, 3, 2, 1, 4, 3, 2, 1, 3, 2, 1, 2. <div align="center">DESCENDING.</div><div align="center">R. H.—2, 1, 3, 2, 1, 4, 3, 2, 1, 3, 2, 1, 3.</div>
C#.	R. H.—2, 3, 1, 2, 3, 4, 1, 2, 3, 1, 2, 3, 4, 1, 3. L. H.—3, 2, 1, 4, 3, 2, 1, 3, 2, 1, 4, 3, 2, 1, 2. <div align="center">DESCENDING.</div><div align="center">R. H.—2, 1, 3, 2, 1, 4, 3, 2, 1, 3, 2, 1, 3.</div>
G# & Ab.	R. H.—3, 4, 1, 2, 3, 1, 2, 3, 4, 1, 2, 3, 1, 2, 3. L. H.—3, 2, 1, 4, 3, 2, 1, 3, 2, 1, 4, 3, 2, 1, 2.
D# & Eb.	R. H.—2, 1, 2, 3, 4, 1, 2, 3, 1, 2, 3, 4, 1, 2, 3. L. H.—2. 1, 4, 3, 2, 1, 3, 2, 1, 4, 3, 2, 1, 3, 2.
A# & Bb.	R. H.—2, 1, 2, 3, 1, 2, 3, 4, 1, 2, 3, 1, 2, 3, 4. L. H.—2, 1, 4, 3, 2, 1, 3, 2, 1, 4, 3, 2, 1, 3, 2.
F.	R. H.—1, 2, 3, 4, 1, 2, 3, 1, 2, 3, 4, 1, 2, 3, 4. L. H.—5, 4, 3, 2, 1, 3, 2, 1, 4, 3, 2, 1, 3, 2, 1.

*Descending, the fingering is the same, except where marked differently

FINGERING OF THE MAJOR ARPEGGIOS.

KEYS C, G, & F.

RIGHT HAND.	Fingering of highest note.	LEFT HAND.	Fingering of highest note.
1st Form.—1, 2, 3, 1, 2 - - - - 5		1st Form.—5, 4, 2, 1, 4 - - - - 1	
2d " 1, 2, 4, 1, 2 - - - - 5		2d " 5, 4, 2, 1, 4 - - - - 1	
3d " 1, 2, 4, 1, 2 - - - - 5		3d " 5, 3, 2, 1, 3 - - - - 1	

KEYS D, A, & E.

1st Form.—1, 2, 3, 1, 2 - - - - 5		1st Form.—5, 3, 2, 1, 3 - - - - 1	
2d " 2, 1, 2, 4, 1 - - - - 4		2d " 3, 2, 1, 3, 2 - - - - 3	
3d " 1, 2, 4, 1, 2 - - - - 5		3d " 5, 3, 2, 1, 3 - - - - 1	

KEYS B & C♭.

1st Form.—1, 2, 3, 1, 2 - - - - 5		1st Form.—5, 3, 2, 1, 3 - - - - 1	
2d " 2, 3, 1, 2, 3 - - - - 2		2d " 3, 2, 1, 3, 2 - - - - 1	
4d " 2, 1, 2, 3, 1 - - - - 3		3d " 2, 1, 3, 2, 1 - - - - 2	

KEYS F♯ & G♭.

1st Form.—1, 2, 3, 1, 2 - - - - 5		1st Form.—5, 3, 2, 1, 3 - - - - 1	
2d ' 1, 2, 3, 1, 2 - - - - 5		2d " 5, 4, 2, 1, 4 - - - - 1	
3d " 1, 2, 4, 1, 2 - - - - 5		3d " 5, 3, 2, 1, 3 - - - - 1	

KEYS C♯, D♭, A♭, & E♭.

1st Form.—2, 1, 2, 3, 1 - - - - 3		1st Form.—2, 1, 4, 2, 1 - - - - 2	
2d " 1, 2, 3, 1, 2 - - - - 5		2d " 5, 4, 2, 1, 4 - - - - 1	
3d " 2, 3, 1, 2, 3 - - - - 2		3d " 4, 2, 1, 4, 2 - - - - 1	

KEY OF B♭.

1st Form.—2, 1, 2, 3, 1 - - - - 3		1st Form.—3, 2, 1, 3 - - - - - - 2	
2d " 1, 2, 3, 1, 2 - - - - 5		2d " 5, 4, 2, 1, 4 - - - - 1	
3d " 1, 2, 4, 1, 2 - - - - 5		3d " 5, 3, 2, 1, 3 - - - - 1	

FINGERING OF THE MINOR ARPEGGIOS.

KEYS A, E, & D.

RIGHT HAND.	Fingering of highest note.	LEFT HAND.	Fingering of highest note.
1st Form.—1, 2, 3, 1, 2 - - - 5		1st Form.—5, 4, 2, 1, 4 - - - 1	
2d " 1, 2, 4, 1, 2 - - - 5		2d " 5, 4, 2, 1, 4 - - - 1	
3d " 1, 2, 4, 1, 2 - - - 5		3d " 5, 3, 2, 1, 3 - - - 1	

KEY B.

1st Form.—1, 2, 3, 1, 2 - - - 5	1st Form.—5, 4, 2, 1, 4 - - - 1
2d " 1, 2, 4, 1, 2 - - - 5	2d " 5, 3, 2, 1, 3 - - - 1
3d " 2, 1, 2, 3, 1 - - - 3	3d " 3, 2, 1, 3, 2 - - - 1

KEYS F♯, C♯, G♯, & A♭.

1st Form.—2, 1, 2, 4, 1 - - - 4	1st Form.—2, 1, 3, 2, 1 - - - 2
2d " 1, 2, 4, 1, 2 - - - 5	2d " 5, 3, 2, 1, 3 - - - 1
3d " 2, 4, 1, 2, 4 - - - 2	3d " 3, 2, 1, 3, 2 - - - 2

KEYS D♯ & E♭.

1st Form.—1, 2, 3, 1, 2 - - - 5	1st Form.—5, 4, 2, 1, 4 - - - 1
2d " 1, 2, 4, 1, 2 - - - 5	2d " 5, 3, 2, 1, 3 - - - 1
3d " 1, 2, 3, 1, 2 - - - 5	3d " 5, 3, 2, 1, 3 - - - 1

KEYS A♯ & B♭.

1st Form.—2, 3, 1, 2, 3 - - - 2	1st Form.—3, 2, 1, 3, 2 - - - 2
2d " 2, 1, 2, 3, 1 - - - 1	2d " 2, 1, 3, 2, 1 - - - 2
3d " 1, 2, 3, 1, 2 - - - 5	3d " 5, 3, 2, 1, 3 - - - 1

KEYS F, C, & G.

1st Form.—1, 2, 3, 1, 2 - - - 5	1st Form.—5, 4, 2, 1, 4 - - - 1
2d " 2, 1, 2, 3, 1 - - - 3	2d " 4, 2, 1, 4, 2 - - - 2
3d " 1, 2, 3, 1, 2 - - - 3	3d " 5, 3, 2, 1, 3 - - - 1

www.ingramcontent.com/pod-product-compliance
Lightning Source LLC
Chambersburg PA
CBHW021631270326
41931CB00008B/962